Welcome to Mexico

by Mary Lindeen

Table of Contents

Consultant:
Adria F. Klein, Ph.D.
California State University, San Bernardino

capstone classroom
Heinemann Raintree • Red Brick Learning
division of Capstone

Hello, Mexico!

"¡Hola!" That is how you say "hello" in Spanish. Spanish is the official language of Mexico. Mexico is a country in North America. It is south of the United States.

Some people think the country of Mexico looks like a tornado. Others think it looks like a triangle. What do you think?

Open Spaces

Mexico has mountains, deserts, and beaches. People like to go swimming and snorkeling in the oceans. People from all over the world visit Mexico's sunny beaches.

There are also many farms in Mexico. Farmers grow corn, beans, fruit, and other crops. The rich soil and warm weather make it a good place to farm.

Fiesta

A **fiesta** is a fun celebration in Mexico. Dancers wear colorful outfits. Musicians play traditional music, and everyone eats their favorite foods.

Breaking open a piñata is another fun thing to do at a fiesta. The piñata is full of candy and toys. Everyone takes a turn hitting the piñata to crack it open.

Tortillas are a kind of flat, round Mexican bread. They can be made from corn meal or wheat flour. Tortillas are often filled with meat, beans, or cheese.

Crispy fried tortilla chips are eaten with **salsa**, another popular Mexican food. Salsa is made by mixing chopped tomatoes, onions, and chili peppers. Salsa can be mild or very spicy.

Art and History

Mexico is also famous for its silver. Silver comes from deep underground mines. Artists use the silver to make beautiful jewelry and decorations.

Mexico is known for other kinds of artwork too. These colorful blankets are just one example of the beautiful art made by the talented artists of Mexico.

Some of the most famous places in Mexico are very old. They are the remains of buildings that are more than a thousand years old. This pyramid was built by the ancient **Mayan** people.

The **Aztec** people also lived in Mexico. Many of their cities were destroyed by explorers and settlers who came to Mexico from other countries. The people of Mexico are proud of their country and its history.

Mexico Today

Mexico has both small towns and big cities, just like any other country. The largest city is Mexico City. It is the capital of Mexico. Millions of people live and work there.

There are many new shops, homes, and office buildings in Mexico City. There are also buildings that are hundreds of years old. It is like the country of Mexico itself. It is a very modern country whose people are also proud of their history.

Glossary

Aztecs	people whose powerful empire ruled central Mexico from the 1300s to the 1500s
fiesta	a celebration or festival held in Spanish-speaking countries
Mayan	belonging to a Native American people of Mexico and Central America
salsa	a Mexican sauce made from chopped vegetables
tortilla	round, flat corn or wheat bread